31 THI

WHICH WILL HELP BOOST YOUR ABILITY TO PICK
GREAT
INVESTMENT FUNDS

&

5 THINGS TO AVOID

To Richard and Debbie

With love and best wishes,

Richard

xx

Richard Jennings

Book design & layout by Velin@Perseus-Design.com

ISBN Number: 978-0-9956348-0-0 (Paperback)

CONTENTS

31 THINGS WHICH WILL HELP BOOST YOUR ABILITY TO PICK GREAT INVESTMENT FUNDS?

5 THINGS YOU SHOULD PROBABLY AVOID WHEN PICKING INVESTMENT FUNDS?

FOREWORD

I believe in the importance of personal finance education. We learn so much at school, but often not enough about the practical things that will help us negotiate our way through life, including personal finance. We now have the foundations of financial education taught in schools so at least we are beginning to address the gap. We should all be able to make the most of our money and in order to do that, we need financial capability. Without financial capability we are vulnerable. In the words of the old saying "If you think education is expensive – try ignorance".

Irrespective of what we achieve in life, money matters and we need to understand how to deal with it. Whether we choose to work with an adviser to help manage our finances or not, we should still understand what is being done in our name.

There was a time when a certain amount of responsibility for our personal finances may have been delegated to someone else without too much thought, but looking back we can see where that has got us, with a recent history of mis-selling and compensation pay-outs. I believe we have moved on from those times though and that we now have access to better tools and knowledge and we are more willing to engage with our finances.

We make many different financial decisions throughout our lives and one of those key decisions is where and how to invest. This book discusses investment funds in accessible language and allows us to understand and engage with investment choices. It explains the many different tools that can be used to evaluate a collective fund and explores the type of due diligence work that an investment adviser would typically carry out on our behalf.

A small investment in this book in terms of time, will pay dividends in understanding some of the myriad choices we have available and the decisions we need to make. At the very least we will be able to engage in an informed discussion with our financial advisers about investment choices.

Jane King FCA BSocSc
Senior Lecturer
Accounting, Finance & Economics
Oxford Brookes University

PREFACE

Investment comes in many forms. From residential property (*buy to lets*), through to equities (*stocks & shares*), woodland, through to commodities, fixed interest instruments (*these will include government gilts, treasury bonds and corporate bonds*), through to more tangible assets such as gold coins, fine wines and vintage cars .... and of course, a great many alternatives in between.

With some £930 billion under management as at July 2016 in unit trusts and open ended investment companies (*hereinafter referred to as OEICs*), plus another £140 billion or so in closed end investment companies (*including investment trusts*), the majority of investors in the UK will use collective investment funds, perhaps via Individual Savings Accounts (*ISAs*), other savings schemes of some kind, insurance company products such as investment bonds, pensions (*typically via personal pensions or self-invested personal pensions*) or investing directly into the funds themselves.

Collective investment funds are basically a way of pooling your money with others to invest into a form of investment arrangement which then benefits from (*amongst other things*), professional fund management, the choice of specialisation in investment sectors or themes, or generalisation and very importantly, **diversification.**

The latter in particular generally recognised as **a key component in reducing investment related risk.**

Given the fact that collective investment funds have become the 'vehicle of choice' for so many investors, my intention with this book has therefore been to concentrate on the medium of such funds. Consequently my words are aimed at you if you wish to know more about some of the mystery that surrounds investing generally and collective investment funds specifically (*and the buying/selling criteria that might help them become better investors*).

It may also assist you if you decided to outsource your investment decisions and portfolio management to investment professionals, but you still wish to be involved in the discussions regarding your investment needs with your advisers and understand more about the methodology adopted by them. Perhaps to help you understand and measure as to whether or not you are getting a decent return on your money, relative to what might be available elsewhere.

Or maybe simply to ascertain whether or not you are getting **value for money** from your advisers.

It is fair to say that **many private investors lack confidence when it comes to making decisions about their investments.** Whether to buy, what to buy, whether to sell, when to sell, whether to seek advice or whether to try and go it alone etc.

Unfortunately many will make investment buying decisions based solely on the marketing skills/advertising copy of the investment groups.

Much attention is given to **past performance**, with perhaps little knowledge as to **how** that performance has actually been achieved. Whether the performance has been **consistent**, what actual **risks** are associated with a given fund, or indeed, whether the **timing** of investing into a certain fund, sector or asset class, has in fact been a major key to that performance.

Conversely, **selling decisions** are quite often made simply by reacting to a particular piece of adverse news-flow, without having the detailed knowledge required as to how that news-flow may affect investments over the medium to longer term. Or indeed, without even having a longer term strategy in place. But such **short term thinking rarely pays off.**

Generally, investment professionals will tell you it is rarely a good idea to run for cover and sell <u>after</u> a market or particular fund has fallen steeply, unless you are absolutely certain that further falls are to follow. After all, by reacting in this way you will actually be crystallising a loss, which before the sale was merely a loss on paper.

Having said that, it is obviously important to get some form of understanding or feel as to why the market or particular fund might have fallen, what has driven the fall and what the future might look like. Indeed it is a fact though that professionals will often use falls in the market to add to their positions, recognising the added value that falls in stock prices have presented them with.

History suggests that **private investors would benefit from a longer term strategy which rides out short term volatility and utilises the principles of diversification.** This is likely to be much more successful than one based on short term, knee jerk reactions to things.

A good example of this was seen in the immediate aftermath of the Brexit vote, in June 2016. The market had rallied a little before the vote itself, on the broadly based expectation of a Remain vote winning through. The success of the Leave vote therefore left many in the UK (*and indeed overseas*) shocked, including those in the city who were clearly not expecting a majority to actually tick the Leave box.

Prices of shares were immediately marked down at opening of the market, by some 10% across the main FTSE100 index and by much more for those stocks whose fortune centred more on the UK domestic economy, such as housebuilders and car distributors.

However by the end of that first day, the index had bounced back from a negative 10% at opening, to finish 'only' 3% down on the day (*a recovery from the day's low point of some 7%*) and in the couple of weeks following, had added another 10% or so. So any investor panicking and selling immediately in the morning of the EU referendum result would have not only actually crystalised a 10% loss, but missed out on something like a 17% recovery in the two weeks following.

The sheer choice of funds available can make things quite bewildering for investors too, particularly those who are somewhat inexperienced. It is therefore understandable why so many investors prefer to hand over responsibility to a financial adviser or investment specialist to make all their investment decisions for them.

.... and such **specialist advisers can indeed be a very valuable resource and the good ones should effectively 'pay for themselves'**, with their fees and costs more than covered by the outcome of their advice and recommendations being seen through to fruition, whether it be through tax savings, or investment performance the investor wouldn't otherwise have enjoyed, were it not for the advice in the first place.

I have long held the belief though, based on some 30 years of experience in managing money for clients, that investors would generally benefit by understanding more of the issues involved in investing. Partly, so that they can make better decisions for themselves. Partly (*where applicable*) so that they can pick investment advisers wisely and consider any professional advice given to them carefully, thereafter making better, informed decisions.

That should hopefully lead to a better outcome for all concerned.

In this book, I have attempted to give you some insight as to the sort of things you should take into consideration when carrying out a due diligence process in choosing an investment fund or funds.

It will also give you the knowledge to be able to ask the right sort of questions to establish the investment credentials and experience of any adviser you are contemplating employing to assist you.

It is not an exhaustive or exclusive list. I have tried to keep things as straightforward as possible, avoiding the jargon of the city where I can, except where I felt it was necessary to describe a particular process, indicator or fact.

It is fair to say that there are other considerations which could be taken into account, especially by professionals as part of their own due diligence process. Where a decision is made by you to outsource investment decisions and/or portfolio management to professionals, I would certainly expect them to be able to subsequently demonstrate to you (*upon request*), that they have at least taken most, if not all, of the factors listed in this book, into account in their own work and deliberations on your behalf. If they can't do that when asked, then you should question as to whether or not you have the appropriate advisers working for you. You will almost certainly get a better outcome by sourcing an **investment specialist**, rather than a, shall we say, more general practice financial adviser.

Investment funds can be acquired through a variety of different products, such as ISAs, pension plans, insurance company investment bonds, as well as being held directly. Each different type of product will have its own tax structure and some will be of benefit to a certain type of client, or a client's particular set of circumstances, more than others. Be very aware though that an incorrect choice of product or route to buying an investment fund itself, could mean you end up paying much more tax than is necessary. You could also end up paying much more in charges!

I do not attempt to analyse the different tax treatment of products within this book, but purely focus on the investment fund selection process and give some assistance to you, where this is appropriate in sourcing an investment professional to guide you.

By absorbing much of the information detailed in this book and then applying it wisely, **you should substantially improve your chances of picking great investment funds.** However it is very important you accept that no amount of analysis can **remove all risks** of investing, nor guarantee success. We simply don't know what we don't know.

For instance just one of the categories of totally unpredictable risk, is **Event Risk**. This is basically the risk of an unforeseen event impacting upon market sentiment generally, or maybe an individual company's profitability and therefore share price. Examples might be acts of terrorism, accidents, or natural disasters such as hurricanes, earthquakes and floods.

Even the most well informed and experienced of investors would not have been able to predict with any degree of accuracy, events such as the major accident on the Deepwater Horizon rig which affected BP in 2010, the accounting problems with Tesco in 2014 or the discovery of the emissions falsifications scandal at VAG in 2015, all of which had a significant negative impact at the time on not only the share prices of those companies affected, but the sectors in which they operated as well as the markets generally.

You must realise therefore that there are no guarantees to successful investing. There is no magic bullet. However, using the principles, technical indicators and techniques described in this book, many of which are used extensively by professional investors, will certainly greatly improve your chances of success.

Richard Jennings

ACKNOWLEDGEMENTS

I would like to acknowledge and give special thanks to Rachel Groves, Marion Shervington and my daughter Hannah Louise, who have all provided considerable technical support and assistance in the production of this book.

Also to my very good friend of many years, Peter Thomson, for his inspiration, motivation and encouragement, to finally get my long held thoughts into publication.

DISCLAIMER

This book aims to inform and educate the reader on certain financial issues. The opinions expressed within represent analysis by the author at the time of preparation. Whilst every effort has been made to ensure the content is accurate, it is impossible to predict all the circumstances it which it may be used. They are given for information only and should not be interpreted or construed as investment advice, nor should actions be taken as a consequence of reading this information, without individual and specific financial advice from a regulated adviser. Any figures referred to in this book may be gathered from various sources and amalgamated and whilst every effort has been made to ensure the content is accurate, none can be warranted to be so. It may represent a snapshot of the situation at the time of writing, may have changed since and should not therefore be relied upon for any investment decisions. Accordingly neither the publisher, author, retailer, nor any other supplier of this book shall be liable to any person or entity with respect to any loss or damage caused or alleged to be caused by the information contained in or omitted from this book. Nothing in this book is a recommendation to buy or sell any investment it may refer to by way of example.

Past performance is not a guide to future performance. The value of an investment as well as the income derived from it, can fall as well as rise and you may get back less than you originally invested. Tax assumptions and reliefs depend upon your particular circumstances and may change, if those circumstances or the laws change. Tax advice which contains no investment element is not regulated by the Financial Conduct Authority. You should read all investment scheme documents carefully before investing and before entering into an investment agreement you should preferably consult a professional investment specialist.

Any links to third party websites within this book are provided in good faith and for information only. Neither the author nor the publisher accepts any responsibility or legal liability for the materials contained in any third party websites referenced in this book and your access and use of such services and materials is at your own risk.

SO, WHAT ARE 31 THINGS WHICH WILL HELP BOOST YOUR ABILITY TO PICK GREAT INVESTMENT FUNDS?

Perhaps the very first question you should be asking yourself is ...

"WHAT DO I ACTUALLY WANT MY INVESTMENT FUND/S TO DO?"

1. DO YOU WANT OR NEED INCOME FROM YOUR INVESTMENTS?

... OR CAPITAL GROWTH?

... OR, PERHAPS, A COMBINATION OF BOTH?

Early on in the investment fund selection process, you should decide whether or not you are seeking income from your investments. Or, maybe just capital growth over the longer term? Or perhaps a combination of both, having some income provision together with the **potential** for an element of capital growth over the long term as well.

Some funds will have little or no intention to produce an income or dividend yield, their mandate being all about achieving capital growth over the longer term.

If income is one of your main objectives, then your focus should be on those funds which have a mandate to pay a regular income to investors. The Investment Association (*hereinafter referred to as IA*) UK Equity Income sector has long been one of the largest and most popular collective investment fund sectors in the market and would be a good starting point for your selection process.

It is also one of the most competitive, attracting some of the country's most successful individual fund managers. Other popular sectors for the income investor to go fishing in, will include the Equity and Bond Income sector, the Corporate Bond sector, the Strategic Bond sector and the Global Equity Income sector. Funds from other sectors will pay an income out to you too, but those I have mentioned are amongst the most popular.

When you start looking at the individual funds in detail, you should ascertain what the actual yield is of the fund that you are considering investing in.

This is roughly translated as being the amount of income that will be paid to you, expressed as a percentage of the investment consideration. So £20,000 invested into a fund with a 3.5% yield, will produce approximately £700 p.a. of income for you to begin with. Remember that any quoted income yield will only be an estimate at the point of investment and is not guaranteed thereafter.

You should also consider what the actual dividend distribution dates are, as this will determine the actual cash-flow from your investments, which could be important to you. Some funds will make their distributions of income to investors monthly, others quarterly, some half yearly. It is rare that an income orientated fund will only make a single distribution per year.

By at least being aware of the payment dates, you could possibly put together a portfolio of different funds, with different distribution dates throughout the year, ensuring that there is a distribution of income to you on a regular basis throughout the whole year.

You should also ensure that you select income units when buying the fund and not accumulation units, the latter being more suited to growth orientated investors and as such will not pay an income to you.

Instead, any distributions or dividends paid by the stocks held within the fund, will be added back in to the overall fund value to effectively increase the unit price of the fund.

Bear in mind that even if you are only seeking capital growth over the longer term, it is still perfectly rational and acceptable to include funds in your portfolio whose main objective is to deliver an income. This is because it is the **total return** which should be the consideration and if there are exceptionally well managed income orientated funds out there, then the total return may be attractive enough to consider holding it in a growth portfolio anyway (*and in those cases, have the income being produced re-invested back into the fund, usually to buy more units in the fund*).

Growth investors generally have a much broader choice of funds to invest in as they can not only fish in those fund sectors which include out and out capital growth funds (*such funds generally being denied to the income investor as they pay little or no dividend*), but they can also consider income funds, perhaps then re-investing the resulting dividends and distributions to achieve a total return which may meet their overall objectives.

THE PRIMARY BASIS OF STOCK SELECTION IN A PARTICULAR FUND

PASSIVE INVESTING OR ACTIVE MANAGEMENT?

Collective investment funds are generally structured in such a way so that they either:

Invest in **all** stocks in a particular index that the fund wants to track. This means that there will be no judgement or decisions made whatsoever as to whether the individual stocks within the particular index are good, bad or just plain ugly.

By way of example, a FTSE 100 index tracking fund will hold every single stock in that index, regardless of the profitability of each company or indeed the desirability of holding same.

This process is generally referred to as **passive investing or index tracking.**

OR

Investment funds can be **actively managed**. Which means someone is actually applying judgement in the whole decision making process as to which underlying stocks should be included, or omitted in a particular fund, as the case may be.

Each method has its relative merits and drawbacks and there should not really be an argument that 'one is better than the other', or even that it is a case of active versus passive. It is not. It is more a matter of active **AND/OR** passive.

There are many fans of passive investing and it is fair to say that this route to investment is generally growing in popularity. Equally there are many advocates of active management who wouldn't dream of just relying on index tracking to seek the gains in their investments that they desire.

Indeed the 'Active' or 'Passive' debate has been touring the investment landscape, ever since passive funds first became widely available in the 1990s. The debate has received increased attention in recent years due to passive investment vehicles becoming more readily available to retail investors. Advocates of the passive route commonly highlight their low cost nature and periods of under-performance by active managers generally.

Active managers on the other hand, highlight the risks of passive investing's exposure to portfolios which can be heavily concentrated in a very small number of sectors (*such as oils, financials or pharmaceuticals*) and that passive strategies which aim to track an index gross of charges, systematically underperform their benchmark, because of the fees that need to be taken into consideration.

The two very different styles can happily sit alongside each other and it is more a question of ascertaining exactly what the investor is seeking and thereafter finding suitability.

A useful analogy is to remember that an active lifestyle is much more likely to lead to a fit and healthy body, compared to taking a sedentary or passive approach to life. However, an active lifestyle also arguably exposes you to greater risks of accident or injury, whether that be falling off a bike, twisting an ankle running or playing tennis, or suffering muscle tears or strains in the gym. I know the latter only too well myself, having had two gym induced injuries in the last few years.

However on balance, generally one is aware of the risks of an active lifestyle and accepts them for the added benefit of the likelihood of a long and healthy life. Having said that, we all know there are still plenty of people who live a long life, despite the fact that they are smokers, drinkers and spend most of their time on the couch in front of a TV.

It's about balance and it's about making personal choices in life.

2. PASSIVE INVESTING

Commonly referred to as index tracking, **Passive investing** is a strategy that aims to match the returns from the stock-market, as measured by a particular or specific index (*such as the FTSE 100 index*) or set of indices.

Passive funds can be easy and quick to trade in and out of. ETFs (*which are a form of index tracker*) for instance can generally be bought and sold throughout the trading day.

In absolute terms, an index tracking fund should follow a market down, as well as up.

By its nature, passive investing involves taking as few 'active' decisions as possible. The type of investor usually attracted to passive investing is not usually concerned with 'above market average' returns on their investments. So this type of investing would be suited to you if you are satisfied simply with earning the market rate of return.

Passive investors may want a 'low maintenance' investment. They may not wish to monitor a fund manager's investment decisions. They may consider they don't have the knowledge to make active investment decisions, or even to select someone to make those decisions on their behalf.

Some of 'The Pros' of Passive Investing

You tend to know what you are getting – You are likely to know what stocks are in your fund (*as they will be the stocks which make up the particular index*) and you know you will generally be getting close to the market return.

It tends to be a cheap and easy way to access the market – One of the main attractions of passive management is that management fees are usually less than for an actively managed fund. This is because an index tracking fund does not have to do any analysis or research as to which stocks to buy. It simply buys whatever stocks are in a particular index.

Likewise, it doesn't need to pay fund managers, research analysts or other support staff, all of whom are typically involved in active fund management. Few decisions need to be made and the manpower involved in running such a fund is therefore substantially less.

There is usually little risk of under-performance – It is unlikely that a passive fund or index tracker will underperform the relevant market by a big margin.

... and some of 'The Cons'

Lack of choice – When you choose a passive fund, you are restricted to investing in a near replication of a particular market index and hence only having the potential to earn the market average rate of return.

Little or no prospect of outperformance – There is hardly any potential for a passive fund to outperform the index it is tracking, over a period of time. Indeed it will almost certainly underperform its associated index, due to the impact of charges being imposed on the fund, albeit usually at a relatively low level.

Lack of diversification – As passive funds try to replicate the stocks in a particular index as closely as possible, they are forced to hold the largest companies and sectors in that index. This means that if an index is made up of a large number of stocks weighted towards a particular sector (*say, oil companies or maybe financial stocks or pharmaceuticals*), the index as a whole will have a bias towards that sector or sectors and so will any fund tracking it therefore, regardless as to whether or not that particular sector is economically the 'right' place to be investing at a given period of time.

There is effectively no human led 'choice' as to what goes into an index. The content of a particular index is dictated by the mandate of the index. So for instance the FTSE 100 is made up of the 100 largest companies in the UK, determined by their number of shares in issue multiplied by the prevailing share price. That fact is not open to debate.

The situation is usually reviewed once per quarter and as companies' size alters over time (*by way of their share price moving up and down*), then some companies will drop out of the index as they are no longer large enough to be part of the 'top 100 club' and others whose share price has increased, will take their place.

By way of an example of this potential *lack of diversification*, in April 2008, 40% of the FTSE 100 index was made up of just two sectors, oils and financials. If either of these sectors performed badly (*as the banks did of course*) this would have had a significant impact on the index as a whole and therefore any fund tracking the index. When the dot.com bubble burst in March 2000, one sixth of a FTSE 100's index tracking fund at that time would have been invested in just one stock, (*Vodaphone*)!

Forced to buy and sell, regardless of 'value' – When the index is 're-balanced', passive funds could be forced to sell stocks leaving the index (*which may actually represent good value because they are at their historical cheapest*) and buy those that are entering (*which conversely, may be at their most expensive historically*). The passive funds also have to keep holding index weightings in stocks and sectors, when they fall as well as rise.

KEY SUMMARY POINT

If costs are of greater consideration to you than the potential for out-performance, then passive investing may be right for you.

3. ACTIVE MANAGEMENT

Active investing is a strategy that aims to beat, not just match, the returns from the stock-market or a particular index. There are many different ways in which actively managed funds can achieve this. Running central to all however is a fundamental belief that using skills and investment processes, it is possible to 'beat' the market.

It is fair to say that the majority of funds in the UK are actively managed. This is generally because investors prefer that their capital is allocated according to the judgment of a skilled investment professional, rather than its fortunes left to the whim of a market index.

Active funds are not tied to the stock or sector weightings of an index. They have specific performance objectives, with fund managers usually selecting stocks according to individual investment strategies.

The managers of active funds can make informed decisions to exploit what they see as the inefficiencies of the market. They can anticipate changes in market conditions and adjust their portfolios ahead of those perceived changes happening.

The potential rewards from active fund management are therefore greater. But I emphasize the word potential as nothing is guaranteed.

If you want to beat the market and are not prepared to simply settle for the average return, then active management may be for you. Active investors usually understand the risks of stock-market investing and that these need to be balanced with the potential returns. They have the confidence and knowledge to set their own investment objectives, often having taken expert advice and they are prepared to pay for the expertise to achieve their aims.

Some of 'The Pros' of Active Investment Management

Real prospect of outperformance – The best actively managed funds have significantly outperformed the market index over the longer term.

Flexibility to move in and out of sectors – Active funds are not tied to the stock or sector weightings of an index. They have the potential to avoid sectors that the fund manager believes may underperform. To try and preserve value in a falling market, they can move out of stocks most likely to suffer (*e.g. perhaps selling insurance related stocks following a major natural disaster*). They can also reduce weightings in entire sectors, or in some cases ignore them entirely. Conversely, they can increase holdings in both stock and sectors when they have a more positive view.

15

Possible to achieve a variety of investment styles and strategies – An active investor can choose amongst many management styles and strategies to best suit his/her investment goals and attitude to risk.

Achieve a broader perspective – Active fund managers will usually take a much broader perspective when investing, looking at the key trends and structural shifts in economies, or consumer behavior that could affect companies' prospects.

... and some of 'The Cons'

Performance likely to depend on the skills of the fund management team – Over two thirds of active managers with a 10 year track record, have unfortunately failed to beat the FTSE All Share Index over 10 years

Actively managed funds have higher costs – Higher costs and management fees (*compared to passive funds*) are required to pay for the extra expertise and resources needed for active managers to make informed stock-picking decisions.

There can be a lot of time and effort involved – An investor needs to put time and effort (*or of course employ a professional adviser to do that*), into researching a range of funds before choosing a particular fund to invest in.

KEY SUMMARY POINT

Great investment funds will usually outperform relevant indices on a consistent basis. Such funds are however in the minority when all collective funds are taken into consideration.

STRUCTURE OF FUND

Investors face a multitude of investment choices these days. The different ways to invest, the different investment products and vehicles to consider and choose from, together with the varying tax treatment of same. There are literally thousands of collective investment funds available to choose from. Choice is determined by several factors, including your individual taxation considerations, your specific objectives, as well as your attitude towards investment risk and your tolerance to or capacity for, loss.

It is fair to say that there are various types of risk associated with different types of products/funds, including (*but not exclusively*) **counter-party risk, gearing risk, liquidity risk, credit risk** etc and some types of products/funds carry a greater number of different types of risk than others. It is also true that the actual legal structure of the fund, whether it be an open ended fund, a closed end fund or perhaps an exchange traded fund, can in itself determine certain types of risk.

By way of example, the **liquidity risk** carried by open ended funds participating in the commercial property sector in particular, came to the fore in the post Brexit environment in the UK in the summer of 2016. A large number of investors thought that Brexit would contribute to a slowdown in the UK economy and that we could also witness many European companies closing their UK based European headquarters and relocating to the continent. Those two fears combined to lead to a deteriorating outlook for commercial property generally and many sought to cash in their property based investments.

Some of the managers of open ended funds specialising in physical commercial property (*as distinctly opposed to property funds investing in the equity of property based quoted companies*) were fearful of not having enough cash or liquidity in the funds to be able to meet the redemption demand and that they would have to start putting properties up for sale in order to raise sufficient liquidity. Selling property when it may not be the best time to do so is rarely a good thing and the whole subject of property conveyancing is such that it can take weeks to complete sales anyway.

Fund management groups therefore decided (*with the full involvement and backing of the regulator*) that they had to act quickly to calm down the fears of investors and most importantly, they had to act to protect the interests of those investors within the funds taking a more pragmatic, longer term view and who didn't want to sell or see the value of their holdings diminished through forced sales, brought about some would argue a knee jerk reaction to a single event.

The fund management groups suspended dealing in many of the funds, meaning that redemptions (*purchases and sales of units*) couldn't then take place, at least until a point in time in the future when the suspensions would be lifted.

This action temporarily eased the pressure on the managers of the property funds to have to sell properties in a forced sale environment and gave them time to go about sales in a more orderly manner, seeking out wherever possible better sale prices than might otherwise have been the case.

The whole subject of commercial property and the fund suspensions also highlighted and reminded investors of the fact that open ended funds (*where units are created and cancelled on a day to day basis to cope with the inflows and outflows of investor monies*), can carry huge liquidity related risks.

This is particularly true in the commercial property sector where of course the very assets the funds are actually investing in, are illiquid ones.

KEY SUMMARY POINT

The way a fund is legally structured can determine the extent to which categories of different types of risks may apply.

4. OPEN ENDED FUNDS (*Unit Trusts/OEICs*)?

Open ended investment funds are usually known as **Unit Trusts** (*hereinafter referred to as UT*) or **OEICs**. Such funds invest in underlying individual equities or other financial instruments, with a view to achieving a specific objective for the fund.

They may restrict themselves to invest only in a specific geographical region or even a single country. They may restrict themselves by stock-market size of the individual equity (*some funds for instance specialise in investing in 'smaller' companies*). They may restrict themselves by only investing in a specific sector, such as financial stocks, energy stocks or maybe healthcare stocks.

However whatever the fund investment restrictions are, this type of fund does not have to limit or restrict the number of shares or units in issue. That's why they are called 'open-ended'. When new investors place money in the chosen fund, new shares or units in the fund are created. Equally when someone redeems their investment, those shares are subsequently cancelled.

Units are normally priced just once per day with both new investments in the fund and cancellations of units in the fund being undertaken at the next valuation point (*which may be later that same day or the next day, depending upon the exact timing of the valuation point and the timing of the purchase or sale deal being done*).

5. CLOSED END FUNDS

The most commonly known closed end funds are **Investment Trust or Investment Company** (*hereinafter referred to as IT*).

These are publicly quoted companies in their own right, listed and traded like any other stock, on a recognised stock exchange. Shares in an IT can be purchased at any time throughout the trading day, with the share price moving in real time, as the demand for shares in the IT 'comes and goes', just like any other quoted equity.

An IT will have raised a prescribed amount of capital at its launch, through an initial public offering, by issuing a fixed number of shares. These shares are purchased by investors in the IT, as stock. No further shares will then be issued by the IT unless they undertake a fund raising exercise such as a rights issue where existing shareholders can subscribe for more stock. However as ITs are listed in their own right on a stock exchange, shares in an IT can be bought or sold at any time after their launch, in the aftermarket in the normal way.

Unlike regular stocks, which represent a share of a specific public company, ITs effectively represent an interest in an underlying portfolio of securities and these will be actively managed by the IT's investment team. In a similar way to open ended funds, ITs will typically concentrate on a specific industry, geographic region, or sector, or indeed a combination of these and other factors.

The share prices of ITs will fluctuate, partly and indirectly in relation to the changing values of the underlying stock holdings in them but directly, according to the supply and demand for the actual ITs themselves.

There is however no specific relationship between the performance of the underlying assets within an IT and the quoted share price of the IT itself. This can lead to the anomaly of IT share prices remaining static or even falling (*as there might be little or no demand for the shares of the IT itself and ultimately the share price of the IT is driven by that demand*), at a time when perhaps the underlying stocks within same and the equity markets generally, are increasing.

In such a scenario, the IT's share price is said to be at a **discount** to the underlying net asset value of the IT. Discounts can narrow or widen over time.

The reverse can happen - IT share prices can increase (*as there is general demand for the shares of the IT itself*), at a time when perhaps the underlying stocks within the IT are not rising as much, remaining static or even falling. In such a scenario, the IT's share price is said to be either at a **premium** to the underlying net asset value of the IT, or, if a discount previously existed, that discount is narrowing.

In the most efficient of scenarios, there is no discount, no premium and the share price of the IT fully reflects the underlying net asset value (*hereinafter referred to as NAV*).

There are additional features and risks associated with this type of investment vehicle, including the IT's ability to borrow money (*known as gearing*) within the IT itself, in order to gain greater exposure to the particular shares in the market that the managers of the IT are buying. This can have a positive influence on the net asset value of the IT when things are going well and share prices are rising. By comparison, open ended funds cannot usually borrow within the fund itself in order to gear up the growth.

Unfortunately though, gearing can magnify losses within the IT when markets are falling. In extreme circumstances, there is also the possibility that banking covenants within the IT can be breached, which can lead to very damaging consequences to investors holding shares in the IT.

Despite these additional risks, ITs can play a significant part in many portfolios. Their costs are usually lower than open ended funds and the gearing as well as the discount/premium situation can be used to advantage.

KEY SUMMARY POINT

Although carrying additional risks, the closed end fund's ability to borrow can potentially increase gains from the underlying portfolio of stocks, than would otherwise be the case.

6. EXCHANGE TRADED FUNDS

An Exchange Traded Fund (*hereinafter referred to as an ETF*) is a marketable security that tracks a specific index or batch of indices, a commodity/ies, a credit instrument/s or a whole basket of assets, very much like an index tracking fund. ETFs trade in their own right on regulated stock exchanges and their prices will therefore fluctuate in real time throughout the trading day.

One of their attractions is that you can use a particular type of ETF to **make money in a falling, as well as a rising market**. In addition ETFs typically have higher daily liquidity, tend to (*although most certainly not in all cases*) have lower charges than open ended collective funds or investment companies, making them attractive to individual investors.

Investors are in fact starting to pour billions of pounds into these products, making them one of the fastest growing categories of investment. Assets under management stood at some £170 billion in July 2016, a rise of 11% over the last year.

As well as buying what are known as 'long only' ETFs (*which in much the same way as long only open ended funds, will make money for investors if the share price of the ETF goes up, but will lose money if the share price goes down*), one can buy **'inverse' ETFs** that track the opposite return of that of the underlying asset.

For example, an inverse ETF tracking say gold bullion would gain 1% in price for each 1% drop in the price of the metal. The reverse would be true with the inverse ETF losing 1% in value for each 1% gain in the price of the metal.

One can also buy **'leveraged' ETFs** where investors seek to gain a multiple return of that of the underlying asset. For instance a 2x gold ETF would gain 2% in value for each 1% gain in the price of the metal itself ... and of course conversely, when things 'go wrong', would lose 2% in value for each 1% drop in price of the metal. **So the risks and rewards are potentially much greater.**

One can go one step further and buy **'leveraged inverse' ETFs** where it is possible to gain 2x or 3x (*for example*) that of each 1% drop in the value of the underlying asset being tracked in the ETF. Whilst capable of making large sums of money in falling markets, such ETFs can quickly destroy investor value if things go wrong and markets and/or securities move in the opposite way to that which was expected.

KEY SUMMARY POINT

ETFs can offer a low cost approach to building core holdings in a portfolio.

PERFORMANCE CONSIDERATIONS

7. ABSOLUTE (OR CUMULATIVE) AND RELATIVE PERFORMANCE

When carrying out research to select an investment, you are constantly reminded by the investment groups and adviser community of the mandatory regulatory statement that *'past performance is not a guide to the future'* ... or similar words.

However I believe you can't simply ignore past performance altogether. It tells us many things but it is important that it is not taken in isolation.

There are different ways of looking at performance itself and ideally one should cross reference between at least two and preferably three different performance parameters. I would for instance recommend the use of **absolute** (*also referred to as cumulative*) **performance** combined with **relative** performance and then ascertaining the consistency of the fund's performance, by looking at it over separate **discrete** periods.

Absolute or cumulative performance will tell us the actual return a fund has made over a given timescale. Ideally it should be compared to the actual return from a benchmark, such as the average of the peer group or sector in which the fund sits, for comparison purposes. It will not however, in isolation, tell us how that performance was actually delivered, how it did **relative** to its peer group, nor how **consistent** was the performance.

Relative performance will tell us how well a fund has done compared to something else, usually a benchmark, an index, or other similar funds in its peer group. But it will not tell us what the overall return has been over a given timescale, nor what the current actual direction of travel is for the fund price, only the direction of travel relative to the price of the item it is being compared to (*usually the sector average or benchmark, occasionally, another individual fund of a similar nature*).

Discrete performance will tell us how well the fund has done in different, specific (*or discrete*) moments in time, usually on a year by year basis. In that way one can ascertain the **consistency of performance** (*see section 8.*). Ideally discrete performance should be compared to the actual return from a benchmark (*such as the average of the peer group or sector in which the fund sits in for comparison purposes*) over the same discrete periods, otherwise the data produced has less or even little meaning. Discrete data about a fund on its own, doesn't tell us whether the fund has outperformed or under-performed though.

In isolation, each of these forms of performance analysis can in fact give potentially give rather misleading information. However when used in conjunction with each other and cross referenced appropriately, they start to build a powerful piece of analysis.

To explain each in turn and illustrate how the data produced from each can build a useful overall picture, I have selected an investment fund at random and analysed it using the three different performance measures above, over the same timescale *(three years to 26th July 2016)*.

The fund I have chosen to do this, simply by way of example, is a generally well respected and in my opinion, well managed fund *(although the fund manager changed in June 2016)*, **CF Miton UK Value Opportunities Fund**, which sits in the IA UK All Companies sector.

The fund was launched in March 2013 and attracted a large amount of investment monies very quickly, as the management credentials of its former fund manager, George Godber, were already well known to investment professionals and quickly became evident to others.

In the three years to 1st August 2016, the fund's 'B' share class *(institutional)* unit price, increased by a highly creditable 42.01%. By comparison, the average return from the sector in which it sits was 16.02%. This sort of significant outperformance will have put it on the radar screen of many investors.

The fund's performance is shown on the chart overleaf by the blue line, with the performance of the sector shown by the red line. One can see graphically that not only did the fund do well in absolute terms over the three year period as a whole, but it comfortably beat its peer group in the process too.

If you were an investor who went into this fund in 2013 or 2014, then you would be very pleased with the return you had during this period.

ABSOLUTE OR CUMULATIVE PERFORMANCE CHART

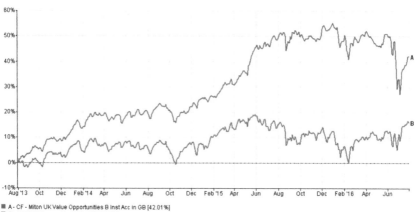

■ A - CF - Miton UK Value Opportunities B Inst Acc in GB [42.01%]
■ B - IA UK All Companies TR in GB [16.02%]

01/08/2013 - 01/08/2016 Data from FE 2016

Source: FE Analytics

It is not that obvious to the untrained eye though whether or not the outperformance was continuous throughout the period or whether or not in fact the fund started to underperform its peer group at any time.

What for instance if you had been thinking about investing into this fund in the spring or summer of 2016?

Questions you might have had at that time could have been:

- *Was the fund still outperforming its peer group?*
- *Indeed was the fund still seeing its fund price grow?*

So let us now look overleaf to the shorter term relative performance chart to see if we can glean further information.

RELATIVE PERFORMANCE CHART

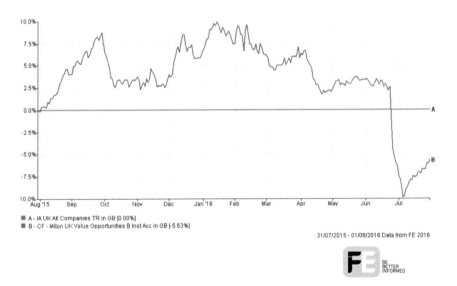

■ A - IA UK All Companies TR in GB [0.00%]
■ B - CF - Miton UK Value Opportunities B Inst Acc in GB [-5.63%]

31/07/2015 - 01/08/2016 Data from FE 2016

Source: FE Analytics

What we have now done is effectively 'flattened' the line representing the performance of the peer group (the IA UK All Companies sector, which is still shown by the red line in the chart above) and then calculated the difference in the performance of that sector with that of the CF Miton fund itself, over the year to 1st August 2016.

The resulting chart looks quite different but gives us data which isn't obvious on the absolute performance chart (*an experienced investor, one who has a good understanding of charts and statistics or a professional investor, will of course still be able to look at an absolute chart and quickly obtain a view on relative returns*).

We can now see (*again from the legend in the bottom left hand corner of the chart*) that, following some three years of exceptional outperformance, the CF Miton fund actually started to underperform its peer group from about February 2016 and over the year to 1ˢᵗ August 2016, **underperformed** its peer group by some 5.63%, with the majority of that underperformance taking place following the EU referendum result.

The sharp fall in relative performance in June 2016 would normally give rise to questions being asked as to 'why' there had been such a reversal in fortunes at that time, following three years of huge success. Was it a one-off type of event, or did it possibly mark the start of a period of under-performance for the fund punctuated by a change in management, with the manager who had been in situ since the fund's launch, George Godber, deciding to go and seek pastures new?.

There can be no doubt that his decision to leave Miton Group (*which was announced to the stock market after trading had closed on 6ᵗʰ April 2016*) was a blow to the investment management company, with the quoted share price of the company falling heavily the day after the announcement.

To be fair though, they reacted swiftly and decisively in appointing a replacement manager with an excellent reputation and track record, to take over the day to day management of the fund.

Personally I believe the fund's unit price value and sharp drop in relative performance had much more to do with external circumstances than the change of management within the fund.

June 2016 coincided with the period covering the EU referendum vote and the subsequent differential performance of stocks following the result of that vote. Sterling fell sharply in the aftermath and there was a belief that the UK could fall into recession, with increased costs from imported goods forcing down profitability and reducing the consumer's ability to spend. Therefore, any UK stocks which were predominantly UK centric or focussed on the domestic economy, were more affected than companies which were far more global in their operations and therefore would have benefitted from the stronger dollar during that period.

Many of the stocks held in this fund held leading up to the referendum were indeed (*and understandably*) focussed on the UK economy and therefore these suffered in the aftermath of the vote result as a consequence of sterling weakening.

The sharp fall in relative performance can I feel be attributed to a UK centric fund understandably holding a good deal of underlying stock focussed on the UK domestic economy, whereas perhaps many of its peer group in the sector at that time may have held stock with good export credentials and therefore benefitting from the stronger dollar at this time.

The quality of the fund's management remains evident as can be seen via the use of discrete performance analysis (*see 8. CONSISTENCY OF PERFORMANCE*).

KEY SUMMARY POINT

Past performance analysis on its own, in the context of fund selection, can be somewhat meaningless and even at times, misleading. It only begins to become useful when used in conjunction with other analysis.

8. CONSISTENCY OF PERFORMANCE

Whilst accepting that it is certainly worth looking at **absolute or cumulative performance** compared to a particular fund's benchmark or sector, (*preferably looking at <u>longer</u> term periods though, such as a minimum of three years or five years*), I do believe that looking at it **in isolation** can be misleading. For instance, a fund could have had one or two 'lucky years' and that could make the cumulative performance to date look good, even over a longer term. But one should also question, how did the fund do in all the other years?

To understand this, you need to look at what is known as the **discrete performance** of a fund. This is the fund's performance within specific periods of time, perhaps on a month by month, quarter by quarter or year by year basis. When used on a relative basis to its peer group (*sector average*) or benchmark, then you will get a good indicator of the **consistency** of a fund manager's performance.

Rather than the use of the linear charts we saw in the previous two examples, I would use a bar chart to look at discrete performance, usually selecting a quarter by quarter basis.

Again by way of example overleaf, I have taken the same fund I used to illustrate cumulative and relative performance, the *CF Miton UK Value Opportunities Fund*.

DISCRETE PERFORMANCE CHART

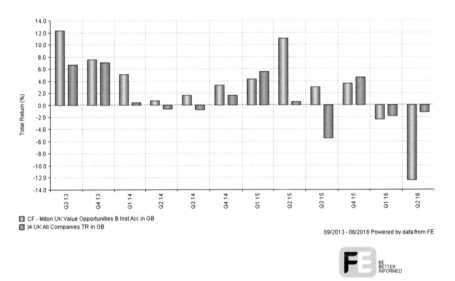

CF - Miton UK Value Opportunities B Inst Acc in GB
IA UK All Companies TR in GB

09/2013 - 06/2016 Powered by data from FE

BE
BETTER
INFORMED

Source: FE Analytics

The bar chart above illustrates the performance of the fund (*again shown in blue*) and compares it to the performance of the sector (*again shown in red*) the fund sits in, each blue or red bar representing a quarter. From this sort of analysis we can ascertain whether the fund manager in question consistently outperformed over the three year period in question or achieved the overall outperformance over the period we talked about before, through one 'lucky' run.

In an ideal world and in general terms, you would want to see the blue bars taller than the red bars on the upper, positive side of the analysis (*i.e. above the '0' total return % line, when the fund is producing positive returns for its investors*) and then the blue bars not falling as much as the red bars on the lower, negative half of the analysis (*i.e. below the '0' total return % line, when the fund is producing positive returns for its investors*).

35

First of all, the chart tells us that in every quarter from Q3 2013 to Q4 2014 (*six consecutive quarters therefore*) the fund outperformed its sector. Even in the two quarters where the sector performance was negative (*Q2 and Q3 2014*), the fund made positive gains for its investors.

The fund underperformed by a modest amount, for the very first time in Q1 2015 and then bounced right back and had another two consecutive quarters of significant outperformance.

In Q4 2015 there was another period of slight underperformance however, then in the very next quarter, Q1 2016, the fund suffered a negative return for the first time since its launch and furthermore the fall was greater than its sector average. In Q2 2016 (*covering the immediate aftermath of the EU referendum therefore*), the fund's performance fell heavily against the sector average.

As I alluded to previously, this would have had much more to do with the fact that the fund had been concentrated on stocks focussed on the UK domestic economy and it was these that suffered more in the wake of the sharp decline in sterling in June 2016.

So in summary, the fund had an excellent run from its launch in March 2013 up to the end of Q3 2015, outperforming its peer group in eight out of ten quarters, which is highly creditable. The fund then struggled from that point in time, in relative terms against its peer group and you can see three consecutive quarters of under-performance compared to its peer group. The fund also had to cope with a change in management during this latter period.

Given the situation identified in the last paragraph, many professional investors might have taken the opportunity to move the fund from their buy list to a holding strategy, probably waiting to see how the incoming manager was going to handle the fund. A few investors might have taken the opportunity of the changes brought about in the aftermath of Brexit, to exit the fund altogether.

KEY SUMMARY POINT

Consistency of performance, not just the actual performance itself, is important to longer term success.

9. PERIODIC RANKINGS

Collective investment funds are usually 'assigned' to a particular 'sector' with other funds of a similar nature (*i.e. all open ended funds that invest in say UK smaller companies, would normally sit in the Investment Association (IA) UK Smaller Companies sector*). Amongst other things, this assignment to specific sectors helps investors make meaningful comparisons between one fund and another.

All funds within that particular sector are then 'ranked' in actual performance terms from top to bottom (*i.e. the fund which is deemed to be the 'best' performing within a particular sector, will be ranked '1.', the second 'best' fund, '2.' and so on. If there were say 80 funds in a particular sector, the 'worst' performing fund would therefore be ranked 80th*). The total number of funds is then divided, perhaps by 100 (*to arrive at percentiles*), sometimes by ten (*to arrive at deciles*) but usually by four (*to arrive at 'quartiles'*).

Using the example quoted above, of a sector with say 80 funds in it and then looking at the quartile rankings of that sector, each group or 'quartile' would have 20 funds in it (*being the aforementioned 80 funds in total in the sector, divided by the 4 groups*).

Looking next at the rankings list, or shall we say, league table from the sector, from the fund ranked '1st', to the fund ranked last at '80th', then those funds which are ranked from performance position numbers '1' to '20' inclusive in the sector league table, would be said to be in the top 25% of all funds in its sector, known as the **top quartile** of that sector, those funds then ranked from league table positions 21 to 40, would be in the **2nd quartile** of that sector, those funds ranked from positions 41 to 60, would be in the **3rd quartile** and finally those funds ranked from positions 61 to 80, would be 4th **or bottom quartile**.

The most desirable quartile ranking group to be in is of course the **top quartile**, with the least desirable being the bottom quartile.

If, rather than looking at quartile rankings (*which means dividing the whole sector into four quarters*), we were to consider decile rankings, then that would mean dividing the sector of 80 funds by ten and each would then be a decile. 80 divided by 10 equates to 8. So any fund in the sector ranking or league table positioned '1' to '8' would be in the top 10% of all funds in its sector, known as the **top decile**. Those funds positioned 9th to 16th would be 2nd decile and so on.

Having grasped the concept of quartile or decile rankings, exactly the same principle applies to percentile rankings. In this case, for a fund to be in the **top percentile** of its sector, it would need to be in the top 1% of all the funds in the sector. Due to the natural volatility of fund prices, percentile rankings are used far less often in the due diligence process.

KEY SUMMARY POINT

Look for consistent top (1st) or 2nd quartile rankings, over different timescales.

MANAGER EXPERIENCE, LONGEVITY & STATUS

10. EXPERIENCE OF THE MANAGER

On the assumption that you have decided upon an actively managed type of fund over a passive investing strategy, I believe that the experience of the individual lead manager of the fund/s to be of significance. For instance, many investment managers working in the city today, haven't even experienced a bear market yet (*such as that seen during the credit crunch*).

In my opinion, experience invariably outshines youth when it comes to investing, partly because the experienced manager will have previously managed money through different economic and trading circumstances and might therefore be better positioned to deal with a particular set of circumstances. However it's also important to ascertain that experienced fund managers are not still living off the reputation of better times long passed.

11. CONTINUITY OF EMPLOYMENT

You should ask *"How long has the manager actually been with their present employer?"* and therefore how much of the fund's performance is actually attributable to the present manager. Many investment managers will make several employment moves during their career. It is fair to say that this is likely to lead to some form of disturbance for their investors, each time they move.

For instance, when a manager leaves a fund you are invested in, you may be faced with the question *"Should I sell my holding and move my money to the new employer of the manager in question?"*. Or stay put?, but risk possible subsequent underperformance from a new manager you may not be familiar with.

12. TEAM APPROACH OR 'STAR' FUND MANAGER?

Some funds are run on a team basis, with no individual singled out as being ultimately responsible for the fund's performance. The majority of funds however will have a specific individual overseeing stock selection and/or asset allocation and many of the more successful funds see their managers rise to 'star' status, attracting media attention and huge remuneration in equal measure. There are merits to both types of fund.

The team approach helps ensure that investors are not left stranded or subsequently suffer under-performance just because a particular manager leaves. The rest of the team carry on with the team process.

However the team approach is less likely to lead to outstanding performance.

'Star' fund managers on the other hand, those perceived to possess something of the midas touch, earn their 'star' status for very good reason.

They will have often demonstrated **consistently good, above average performance** and it is this which will have put them on the 'radar screen' of investment advisers, fund analysts, the media and investors alike. Such performance will usually attract new investors in their droves, thus expanding the funds under management of the employing investment management group, increasing the fees charged by the group to the fund (*as investment management fees are nearly always a percentage of the value of the fund. As the fund grows in size, so do the fees earned by the investment managers, in £s*) and thereby increasing profitability. Which in turn gives them greater scope to reward the fund manager appropriately!

Investment management groups however can sometimes view the 'star manager' culture as a threat to their own business model, as such managers tend to be very aware of their status and demand expensive salary/bonus packages to remain, knowing that if they were to leave, assets under management, could follow the manager out the door.

With this in mind, more and more investment management companies seem to be looking to develop a team based approach to help mitigate future problems of potential asset migration along with the associated 'disturbance' to the investors.

KEY SUMMARY POINT

Regardless of whether or not the fund under analysis is managed by a 'star' fund manager or adopts a team led approach, as an investor I am always keen to learn whether or not the manager of those running the fund have any of their own money invested in the fund. If so, roughly what proportion of their own wealth and if not, ascertain why not.

FUND SIZE

13. SIZE MATTERS!

Not the size of the fund managers! ... but the size of the fund or funds they manage, can certainly impact upon returns in some cases. This is particularly true of open ended funds such as unit trusts and OEICs. Very large funds can sometimes find it difficult to alter strategic positions quickly.

Smaller funds can certainly be more 'nimble on their feet'.

Imagine for instance, a particularly large boat inching its way up the River Thames at the same time as say, a small speedboat. Then suddenly, spotted ahead is an unexpected problem. There is a need for both vessels to change direction as quickly as they can. Which do you think would be able to change direction the quickest? The answer is of course obvious and the analogy applies well to collective investment funds.

A smaller fund can change direction, out of one position or sector and into another, more easily and therefore much more quickly, than say a very large fund.

Take for instance a popular fund such as *Invesco Perpetual High Income Fund*. The fund's factsheet indicated that as at 31st July 2016, the fund had some £11.6 billion invested in it, making it one of the largest funds of its type. Some 5% was invested in British American Tobacco (BAT) which means some £580 million of the fund was invested in this stock, which is a sizable investment by anyone's stretch of the imagination. If for any reason the fund manager decided to exit the stock quickly, then a sale of that magnitude could in itself shift the price of the stock downwards. To avoid being hit with a lower price, the manager could decide to ease out the stock over a period of time, but of course that strategy would also carry risks.

With a large fund which is rapidly expanding in size, it is generally advisable to have a 'feel' for what the fund manager considers to be the fund's optimum capacity. Some managers will have in mind a size for their fund, beyond which they may not feel as confident in being able to continue to deliver competitive returns, perhaps because their **high conviction** relating to particular stocks might be diminished by being forced to add other stocks (*as their fund grows in size*), where they might have **less conviction**.

KEY SUMMARY POINT

There is no hard and fast rule about fund size. It depends on the constraints facing each fund's style and the sector they operate in. There are some well managed large funds and some smaller funds which have a poor performance record. It is just something which needs to be taken into consideration.

INVESTMENT STYLE

In general terms, an investment 'style' can be described as the principle methodology adopted by the different managers of particular collective investment funds, in the way they go about selecting stocks or other assets within those investment funds.

A particular style could be 'value' based or 'growth' based. It could adopt a 'top down' approach or be 'bottom up'. The fund can be focussed on just investing in smaller companies, referred to as 'small cap' (*which basically means a relatively small company in stock market capitalisation terms. See section 16. Market Capitalisation*) or 'large cap'. Or indeed, a combination of these.

It could be 'momentum driven', which essentially means one is following a trend. Sometimes the trend can be a good friend.

….. or use one or more of a variety of other styles.

The different terms used to describe style are sometimes obvious, sometimes less so. This can naturally lead to confusion for some investors.

It is important that investors understand a particular investment manager's style as different periods of time in the economic cycle can suit certain styles better than others. Indeed one can even go so far as to say that being in a certain style of fund at the wrong time in the economic cycle for that particular style, could be quite damaging to investors' value.

Furthermore, unfortunately funds are not always clearly 'labelled' as to whether the fund managers adopt a particular style based approach to their management and stock selection. It is down to fundamental research to ascertain this.

14. GROWTH OR VALUE INVESTING?

Two of the most commonly used investment styles are what is known as either a value approach or a growth approach to stock selection. Both styles of management aim to achieve the best returns for their investors, albeit each goes about things in quite a different way.

Growth Based Funds

Growth funds tend to focus on individual stocks that the funds' managers believe will experience faster than average growth. In other words, there is a fundamental belief that the stock being selected has the potential to grow. Many growth orientated companies are also more likely to reinvest profits back into the business, rather than pay out dividends to shareholders.

Dividend yield may not therefore not a particular concern to a growth manager. Indeed, many so called growth stocks may not even have any earnings at all, let alone a dividend record. It is the potential growth in the company which attracts investors.

So such funds would not really be particularly suitable if you are seeking an income from your investments.

Growth funds also tend to do well in rising markets, but may often under-perform when markets are falling.

KEY SUMMARY POINT

Growth investing may require you to have a higher tolerance to risk.

Value Based Funds

Value based funds seek out individual equities for inclusion in the funds, where the fund manager believes the market has under-valued the company. To arrive at what might be an assessment of an over-valuation or an under-valuation, it will be necessary for the manager to employ intrinsic and relative valuation methods, based on technical and fundamental analysis.

Typically value investors (*including the fund managers of 'value based' funds*) will select stocks with perceived lower than average price ratios, such as price to earnings ratio (*often referred to as the PE ratio*) with a lower than average PE being deemed better 'value' than say a stock in the same sector with a higher PE.

There are however lots of considerations around PE ratios which need to be understood before acting upon them. Value based investors may also look for stocks with much higher than average dividend yields, this again can be an indicator (*but only an indicator*) of value.

It is very important to note that there is no 'correct' intrinsic value of a particular stock. Different investors are likely to apply differing valuation criteria on the same stock and it is this sort of activity which in itself determines a market. One investor may see 'value' and will want to 'buy' or at least 'hold', whereas another investor won't see value at all and will either not want to buy it in the first place, or will want to 'sell' if the stock is already held.

One of the highest profile proponents of 'value' investing is Warren Buffett. Without a doubt, one of the world's most successful investment managers. But there have been plenty of times when even the great man has 'got it wrong'.

An average company (*or collective fund*) can actually become an excellent investment, if bought by you at the right price and then held for a sensible period of time. Conversely a company (*or collective fund*) with an excellent reputation and past performance, can turn out to be only a mediocre investment for you, if too high a price is paid for it to begin with.

KEY SUMMARY POINT

'Value' is a subjective rather than an objective measure.

15. 'TOP DOWN' OR 'BOTTOM UP' APPROACH?

This is another aspect of stock selection or manager style, driven by the concept and belief that it is <u>either</u> the **general prevailing economic and/or market conditions** (*either in a particular sector or geographic region*) that determine the direction of travel for individual stock prices (*Top Down or Macro Driven*), **OR** they are driven mainly by events or the outlook/prospects at the **individual stock level**, regardless of prevailing economic conditions (*Bottom up*).

<u>Top Down</u>

This is a situation where the fund is constructed by <u>primary</u> reference to the overall economic climate, deciding which geographical region or sectors might do well in a certain set of economic conditions first and <u>then</u> finding stocks within those sectors, which might suit the fund's overall purpose and mandate. One might use the expression that the fund manager is looking at the overall 'big picture' to determine asset allocation and that is generally what is referred to as a 'top down' approach.

The economic backdrop generally determines the structure of the portfolio.

Bottom Up

If however the fund's stock selection process is very much based on the fund manager finding what he/she believes to be the right stocks to populate the portfolio, where the fund manager may have a high level of conviction for a particular stock and there is far less concern about the over-riding economic or market backdrop, then this approach is what is colloquially known as a 'bottom up' approach.

Stock selection has priority over the prevailing economic conditions. There might be the belief that certain stocks have the capability to perform well, even if the economic outlook is maybe not looking so kind.

16. MARKET CAPITALISATION – 'SMALL CAP', 'MID CAP' OR 'LARGE CAP'?

The market capitalisation (*hereinafter referred to as MC*) of a company is essentially its stock market worth as opposed to its book value, the latter being determined by reference to its audited accounts and balance sheet valuation.

The MC on the other hand will be calculated by multiplying the number of shares that are in issue, by the current market price of the share. As the share price is likely to be moving up or down throughout the trading day, so does the MC alter. Investment professionals tend to pay a greater significance to the MC than the balance sheet value of a company, when determining the company's size. It is colloquially referred to as the 'market cap'.

By way of an example, if a company has say 50 million shares in issue and the share price is £10 then the company's MC would be £500 million. Its actual balance sheet value, as presented by its accountants and auditors, could be something quite different.

The market then breaks down the MC into three broad categories:

- Large cap' (*short for large capitalisation*) and generally the largest quoted companies in the index, probably with an MC in the region of £5 billion or more. Large cap' companies are the likes of Barclays, Glaxo Smithkline, Sainsburys, Microsoft, Apple, etc

- Mid cap' (*short for middle sized companies in terms of their MC*) being those quoted companies in the middle range size wise, between large companies and small companies and probably with an MC in the region of £1 billion to £5 billion

- and small cap' (*short for smaller sized companies in terms of their MC*), being those quoted companies with an MC of less than £1 billion (*which as you will recognise, is still a rather large company in many ways*).

There is a further MC term heard less frequently, known as micro cap' and this generally relates to those quoted companies at the smaller end of the small cap' range, maybe those with an MC of £150 million or less.

The MC parameters in terms of size are not however set in stone and what is referred to as mid cap' for one investment professional, may be deemed either a small cap' or a large cap' by another. They should be viewed as being general rather than specific categorisations therefore.

Company size can be a determining factor though when making asset allocation decisions. A recognised key to help reduce risk in an investment portfolio is diversification. Such diversification is likely to be determined at the MC level amongst other things. So a portfolio might have a mix of large cap, mid cap or small cap funds. Or it might be that prevailing economic conditions are generally seen to favour one particular MC range. It is a huge generalisation but smaller MC stocks for instance tend to be those whose market is the domestic market.

Large cap stocks on the other hand are more likely to have greater international exposure.

The differences became particularly apparent in the aftermath of the Brexit vote, where those quoted companies with a large international (*and particularly US*) exposure (*most likely to be found amongst the companies with a large MC*), did well as sterling weakened/dollar strengthened and their share prices increased markedly. Those companies more exposed to the UK domestic market (*such as housebuilders and car distributors and more likely to be found amongst companies in the small cap' or mid cap' sectors*) and prone therefore to the increased costs brought about by a weaker sterling (*which of course increases the costs of imported raw materials*), saw their share prices fall sharply.

So an awareness of the MC range within a portfolio might have allowed portfolios to be positioned accordingly.

MCs can also be used as an **indicator of value**.

If for instance a company has a book (*audited balance sheet*) valuation of say £1 billion but for a variety of reasons, the stock is out of favour with the market, then its MC might be only £800 million. This technically (*and very basically*) would suggest that the shares are good value as £1 billion of assets could be acquired for only £800 million. Such a scenario might well make the company the target of a takeover bid, when an acquirer could subsequently 'unlock' value

Small cap' stocks tend to offer the greatest growth potential and historically over the longer time scales have significantly outperformed large caps', but they are also likely to carry greater risks. Their shares are not traded in the same volumes as say large caps and therefore the spreads (*the difference between the buying price of shares and the selling price of shares*) tend to be greater.

Furthermore spreads can open up significantly in times of general market weakness and a rough rule of thumb is that the smaller the company, the greater the spread might be.

Large caps tend to offer more stable returns over the longer term, but their growth prospects may not be as great. Small cap stocks are, by nature, more likely to see much greater volatility in the share prices and are therefore deemed 'riskier'.

There are incidentally some very well-known companies which are not quoted at all and their ownership is still in the hands of a select few, rather than being available to the public generally. Some well-known companies still in private hands and not quoted on the stock market include, Aldi, JCB and Jaguar LandRover.

17. MOMENTUM DRIVEN INVESTING

Momentum investing is yet another investment style. The simple thinking behind this strategy is that investments which have historically done well and whose stock price is continuing to gather momentum, are likely to continue to do so, as further investors pile in to a stock which they see is already 'on the rise'. Momentum investing can to a certain extent be self-fulfilling therefore. As more investors dive into a stock which is increasing in value, the additional buying can in itself help to drive the price higher, particularly if a collective fund doing the buying is substantial in size, as the unit weighting in a stock could be tens or even hundreds of millions of pounds.

It is course rather important for a fund manager, adopting a momentum driven approach, to have a good indication of when the momentum is likely to slow or stop altogether!

18. STYLE ROTATION

This is merely part of the overall process of risk diversification within fund management.

In a similar way as to how different asset classes, such as equities, fixed interest instruments (*debt*), commodities and cash etc behave differently at different points in time, so do the different investment styles employed by managers.

For instance, there will be times when it makes sense to be investing in value based, small cap stocks, rather than say growth orientated, large cap stocks. These periods in time will generally rotate, hence the term style rotation.

TECHNICAL RATIOS

The correct use of technical data can be a very useful part of the fund selection due diligence process. There are scientific ways to establish for instance, which investments carry more risk than others, which are likely to add value over and above the broader return from the market itself, which are likely to go up or down by more than the market.

Understanding the technical ratios and indicators and then applying the data produced from them in an intelligent way, can be a major boost to improving the satisfaction you are likely to derive from your investment portfolio.

It is fair to say though that all **technical ratios and indicators provide rear facing data only.** By that I mean they are based on known facts as to the way investments have behaved in the past. They will not give you any form of guarantee that the behaviour of the past will be replicated in the future. An indication yes, but a guarantee, no. As such **they should be seen and used as a guidance only.** A very useful form of guidance admittedly but nevertheless not much more than that.

19. ALPHA

Without a doubt, alpha is one of the more significant technical indicators used by professional investment specialists.

In a rising market it has been said by some that even a monkey could pick a winning fund (*as of course the majority of funds will be going up in value, broadly at the same time*).

But how can you tell if a particular fund manager is actually adding value to your portfolio, over and above the market return? How can you tell whether you have a found a skilful fund manager? Or just a 'lucky monkey'?

That's where alpha can be of help to you.

It is a formula which effectively measures an investment manager's skill in achieving (*or not as the case may be*) additional returns over and above a suitable market index or fund's benchmark.

Generally, the higher the alpha, the better the manager is doing relative to the market.

However a high alpha score <u>in isolation</u> does not necessarily mean fund manager skill. It could be that manager has enjoyed a short period of good luck. This is where 'Consistency of Performance' comes in (*see note 4.*)

KEY SUMMARY POINT

If a fund shows consistently high alpha, has consistently outperformed its peers and has consistently seen lower than benchmark levels of risk or volatility .... Then, you may have just found a great fund!

20. BETA

Another very important technical indicator to aid successful investing, beta is a scientifically calculated measure of sensitivity a fund might have to market movements generally.

A fund with a beta higher than 1, means that its unit price movements are likely to be in the general direction of the market, but to a greater extent, up or down. So a fund with a beta of say 1.2 is very likely to see its unit price rise or fall by MORE than the market. A fund with a beta of say 0.8 will rise or fall by less than the market.

KEY SUMMARY POINT

If you are somewhat risk averse, it may be sensible for you to generally seek out funds with a lower beta.

21. INFORMATION RATIO

Unlike other technical ratios, such as the Sharpe and Sortino ratios (*see pages 73 and 75*), which focus on returns over the risk free rate, the Information ratio (*hereinafter referred to as IR*) examines the risk adjusted returns achieved relative to a defined benchmark. As such, it offers an insight into the 'active return' achieved by an investment. This is achieved by dividing the return by the **tracking error**. This is a measure of how much risk of an investment fund or portfolio has come about due to active decisions made by the manager.

The tracking error indicates how closely a fund or portfolio follows the index to which it is benchmarked. The measure should therefore reveal how much of a return is generated by taking decisions away from the benchmark. A positive IR indicates it was worthwhile deviating from the benchmark, whereas a negative result suggests that it was not.

Some of 'The Pros' of using the Information Ratio as a Measure of Risk

• For an investment such as an equity fund, the IR helps an investor understand whether it was wise to buy an actively managed fund over a passive (*index tracking*) fund.

• The measure is helpful in defining fund manager skill by showing whether it was worthwhile for the manager to make active decisions.

69

... and Some of 'The Cons'

- The focus on a benchmark means the measure does not help an investor gauge the absolute value of the investment as an alternative to the risk free rate.

- Some argue that IRs will be higher for funds operating in less efficient markets, making it difficult to compare these across sectors or asset classes.

22. MAXIMUM DRAWDOWN

Maximum drawdown is perhaps the simplest measurement of risk. It just looks at the most an investment has fallen by from peak to trough over a fixed period of time. It effectively shows how an investment performed in its worst period.

Some of 'The Pros' of using Maximum Drawdown as a Measure of Risk

- A simple focus on the most that capital could have been lost by choosing a particular investment

- An emphasis on the worst period of time

... and Some of 'The Cons'

- The measure does not capture how quickly or consistently the drawdown (*or loss*) was subsequently recovered by the investment.

- The measure reveals nothing about how effectively an investment has grown during periods of positive absolute performance.

23. R-SQUARED

R-squared is a statistical measure that represents the percentage of a fund's movement in price, which can be attributed to the fund's benchmark.

R-squared values range from 0 to 100. An R-squared of say 100, means that all movements of the fund are completely explained by movements in the index. A high R-squared (*say between 85 and 100*) indicates the fund's performance patterns have been broadly in line with the index. A fund with a low R-squared (*say 70 or less*) doesn't act much like the index.

The R-squared value also has a bearing on the **beta**. A higher R-squared value will indicate a more useful beta figure. For example, if a fund has an R-squared value of close to 100 but has a beta below 1, it is most likely offering higher risk-adjusted returns. A low R-squared value on the other hand, say of 40, would suggest that only 40% of the portfolio's movements can be explained by movement in the benchmark or index. In these circumstances, a beta score to assess the fund's sensitivity to movements in the index would be somewhat irrelevant as so little of the fund is attributable to the index anyway.

KEY SUMMARY POINT

A lower R-squared value means that it is better to ignore the beta as there would be far less correlation with the index and under these circumstances, beta becomes somewhat less meaningful.

24. SHARPE RATIO

The Sharpe ratio is an intuitive way to help understand risk in a portfolio. It is a measure of calculating the risk adjusted return of an investment and can therefore determine whether an investment's return was mainly due to the skills of the fund manager or as a result of taking on excess risk. Rather than focus on how an investment performs when compared to a particular benchmark, the Sharpe ratio looks at its performance relative to 'risk free' returns. Traditionally these have been the returns from US Treasury bills. As such, it attempts to be a true measure of the absolute value of the risk taken in a portfolio.

The ratio is calculated by taking the portfolio total return, deducting the risk free rate *(the resulting figure of this is known as the risk premium)*, then dividing by the standard deviation of the investment.

Some of 'The Pros' of using the Sharpe Ratio as a Measure of Risk

• Focuses on the real impact of moving away from the risk-free rate

• An intuitive way to understand risk

… and Some of 'The Cons'

• Following the credit crunch, many wonder whether the risk free rate as it has classically been defined *(such as the yield on 10 yr US Treasury bonds)*, really is 'risk free'.

- The Sharpe ratio penalizes upside and downside volatility equally. Many investors however are willing to accept some positive volatility.

KEY SUMMARY POINT

The greater the value of the Sharpe ratio, the more attractive is the risk adjusted return.

25. SORTINO RATIO

The Sortino ratio is based upon the Sharpe ratio but is adjusted to only 'punish' an investment for downside volatility. Over the longer term for global equities, the Sortino ratio has been shown to produce relatively similar results to the Sharpe ratio.

Some of 'The Pros' of using Sortino Ratio as a Measure of Risk

• The measure focuses on the downside volatility of an investment

• It retains a focus on returns over the risk-free rate.

… and Some of 'The Cons'

• The complexity of the measure can make it particularly difficult to explain to clients.

• When looking at long term asset class performance, the measure has historically offered little differentiation from the Sharpe ratio.

26. VOLATILITY

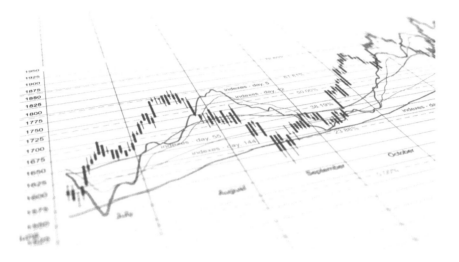

This is another technical indicator to which much attention is paid by professional investment specialists. The volatility of a fund's unit price, the 'jumpiness' of it shall we say, is a standard measure of risk. It is usually measured by standard deviation (*hereinafter referred to as SD*).

The higher the volatility (*the extent of the price moves up and down*), **the higher is said to be the risk of the fund.** High volatility could obviously mean higher returns but could also equate to higher losses when things go wrong.

If a fund for instance has an average return over a given period of 4% and a SD of say 6, it is suggesting that the range of returns has been between minus 2% and plus 10%. A fund with a higher return over the same period, of say 8% but with a higher level of SD of say 12, would have seen returns varying between minus 4% and plus 20%.

Some of 'The Pros' of using SD as a Measure of Risk

- A SD can help 'ordinary' investors understand how they would feel if they received a 'normal' dispersion of returns from an investment.

- It is a good gauge of the consistency with which an investment can deliver returns.

... and Some of 'The Cons'

- Investments certainly do not always deliver a standard distribution of returns and the measure can offer a false expectation of a normal spectrum of outcomes.

- SD penalizes an investment if it achieves strong positive discrete performance, as well as pronounced negative performance within a discrete period.

KEY SUMMARY POINT

Volatility can have huge impact on the longer term returns and should be given serious consideration when constructing a portfolio.

27. VALUE AT RISK

The Value at Risk (*hereinafter referred to as VAR*) is an attempt to create a risk metric that can offer a forward looking estimate of the probability that a portfolio will experience a specified loss over a given period of time.

For example, a portfolio with a one day 5% VAR of £50,000 would suggest it has a 5% chance of experiencing a loss of £50,000 over one day, assuming nothing was done to alter the portfolio.

It is a measure that has come under sustained attack since the credit crunch. In particular, Nassim Taleb, author of ***The Black Swan: The Impact of the Highly Improbable***, argued that it sought to estimate the risk of events that were rare and therefore impossible to predict, but nevertheless did actually occur. He argued that it could give false confidence about an investment.

Some of 'The Pros' of using Value at Risk as a Measure of Risk

- It seeks to be forward looking, whereas many measurements of risk are based on historical statements of fact.

- It can estimate the actual sum of money at risk.

... and Some of 'The Cons'

- The credit crunch exposed the difficulty of predicting unusual events.

- As advisers, we do not really think it is appropriate to give clients forward estimations as to levels of risk as they can be (and indeed are likely to be) inaccurate from day one, due to unforeseen events.

EXTERNAL ASSESSMENTS

28. FUND MANAGER RATINGS

There are a number of rating systems, such as Citywire, FE Analytics, Morningstar, Square Mile etc.

Ratings assessments tend to examine a number of things including (*but not always*) the performance of the individual fund managers throughout the course of their career, looking at their stock picking skills, consistency of performance and the ability of the manager to perform in falling as well as rising markets. They will also assess the risk the manager is taking, relative to the actual performance.

An analysis of the fund manager as opposed to the fund itself will usually be entirely quantitative in nature and be based mainly on the use of the Information Ratio, this being a recognised measure of risk adjusted return.

However you should be aware that the majority of ratings agencies charge the investment management groups to produce the ratings, which can lead to a situation where the ratings are more valuable to the investment management houses themselves, to use in their marketing, than they are to investors.

KEY SUMMARY POINT

A rating is only an indication and usually a subjective one at that, of a particular manager's past performance record.

CHARGES

29. FUND CHARGES

In theory and in an ideal, purist world, investment funds with lower costs should outperform those with higher costs. In reality this is not always the case. Indeed many of those funds with lower than average annual management charges (AMC) rarely head the fund league tables.

Having said that, I believe it is important that you should know exactly what the costs are of a particular fund/s you are thinking of investing in and once you have a shortlist of funds you want to invest in, then filtering them by cost towards the final analysis an indeed be a useful exercise.

To exclude funds on costs though, particularly at say the beginning of a screening process as some might advocate, could actually mean missing out on a fund which has the potential to offer spectacularly good performance returns, just because they are more expensive than others.

A good example of this might be Terry Smith's **Fundsmith Equity Fund**, which sits in the IA Global sector. The AMC of the fund, at 0.9% p.a., is amongst the highest in the fund's sector (*the average AMC of the sector is in the region of 0.75% p.a.*). If a 'cost' filter was done early on in the due diligence process, to effectively get rid of all the 'expensive' funds, then this fund would have been 'confined to the scrapheap' without further consideration.

Big mistake!

This is because over the last year (*to August 2016*) it was actually the best performing fund (*even after taking into account the higher AMC*) in the entire sector (*the Global sector*) of 252 funds that it sits in.

Indeed the fund's performance (*shown by the blue line on the chart overleaf*) over the last five years was over 163% in real terms (*equivalent to an annualised average growth rate of over 21% p.a. compound*), compared to that average for the sector (*shown by the red line*) of just over 54% (*equivalent to an annualised average growth rate of nearly 9% p.a. compound*).

A remarkable performance which placed it firmly at the number one ranking in its sector and in my opinion, thoroughly justifying the additional AMC being charged.

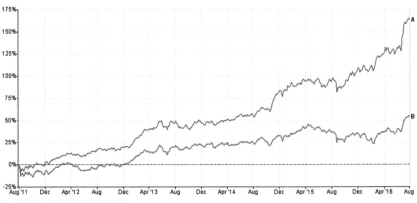

■ A - Fundsmith - Equity I Inc TR in GB [163.35%]
■ B - IA Global TR in GB [54.69%]

01/08/2011 - 01/08/2016 Data from FE 2016

BE
BETTER
INFORMED

Source: FE Analytics

KEY SUMMARY POINT

The thorny issue of charges should be considered, but perhaps only in the final analysis. Filtering out funds just because they have higher charges, could turn out to be a false economy in the long term.

TIME OR TIMING?

30. TIME IN THE MARKET?
OR TIMING OF THE MARKET?

Investing in equities generally can be very rewarding but stock markets inevitably go through periods of uncertainty, perhaps due to a general decline in economic growth or other geo political issues, such as an unexpected change in government or legislation, or perhaps terrorist activity or a natural disaster.

When the twin towers were brought down on 9/11, the US market closed for four trading days, the longest closure since the Great Depression of the 30s. The market re-opened sharply lowered but then recovered much of those early losses, in the months following.

We now seek to examine whether or not it is the length of time that one remains in the market, or trying to get the timing right which is likely to lead to the best outcome.

Time

The length of time investments are held for is probably one of the most important factors to consider, if you want investment success.

Analysis of returns from the FTSE All Share Index over the last 10 years, suggests that had you held the investment for only one year, you would have lost money in over 20% of the instances. However, if you held the investments for a minimum of five years, those losses would have fallen to 15% of the instances and if you held the investments for a minimum of ten years, you would have lost in less than 2% of the instances. It follows therefore that **the longer the term you hold an investment for, the greater is the chance of investment success.**

Of course calculating how much one would make would depend on **when** you invested. It is a fact that stock markets suffer short term fluctuations and sometimes those fluctuations can be severe. However statistics suggest that **your interests as an investor are best served if you hold investments for at least five years and preferably longer.**

Long term investing is not however a way of removing **all risks** of course. The economy can change dramatically over the course of a few years. You must be willing to change your investments if the circumstances around **why** you invested in the first place have changed materially. However I would advocate trying to ignore day to day volatility (*which is a normal part of investment*) and keep to a long term focus.

Make the fundamentals of an investment more important than any prevailing sentiment towards the market generally, or a fund specifically. Remember … sentiment can change on the wind!

KEY SUMMARY POINT

The statistics suggest that the longer the time you remain invested, the greater is the chance of you making money.

Timing

It is a characteristic of human nature that we are much more likely to get emotional when there is the possibility of losing money, than when there is the opportunity to make money. When emotion (*sentiment*) dominates rather than fundamentals, then that is a time when the markets remind us that fear and greed are very much part of the psychology of the market. It is a normal reaction that when markets fall substantially, some investors are drawn to follow the herd, perhaps abandoning their longer term strategy (*if indeed they had one*). **High levels of volatility tend to be news driven and are short lived.**

Astute investors looking at a bigger picture and focused on the longer term will however generally recognise when fear or even panic has set in and will often move to snap up bargain priced investments, at the expense of those who have just dumped their investments at any price, to avoid further potential losses.

That partly accounts for the fact that it is quite common to see large falls in markets followed by large rises and vice versa.

Trying to get the timing right can mean crystalising losses and missing out on the first few days of recovery *(because again it is natural for investors to tend to wait until they've seen a few days of upward movements in the market before they determine that any recovery is actually under way)*.

This strategy can actually have quite an impact on the long term returns, as illustrated by the tables overleaf.

THE EFFECT OF MISSING THE BEST PERFORMING DAYS IN THE UK FTSE ALL SHARE MARKET, OVER THE LAST 15 YRS

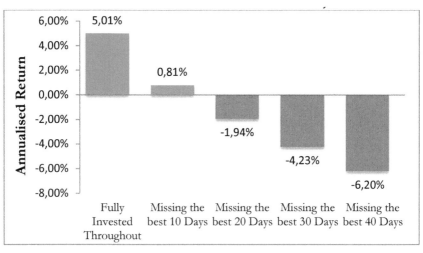

Annualised return based on the performance of the FTSE All Share 30/03/2001 – 31/03/2016 with net income reinvested.

As you will see from the chart overleaf, similar data from the US market, suggests that this situation is not unique to the UK.

THE EFFECT OF MISSING THE BEST PERFORMING DAYS IN THE US S&P 500, OVER THE LAST 15 YRS

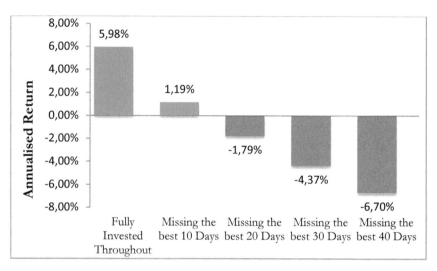

Annualised return based on the performance of the S&P 500 30/03/2001 – 31/03/2016 with net income reinvested.

A key to successful investing is to resist the natural temptation to try and get the timing right and instead, adopt a longer term strategy which rides much of the day to day, week to week volatility of the market.

Overall, the data suggests that **getting the timing of the stock market right is extremely difficult** and the best approach is often achieved by remaining in the market and **sticking to a long term strategy.**

KEY SUMMARY POINT

Statistics back up the theory that <u>time in the market</u> has a greater significance to long term success, than trying to get the <u>timing</u> of entry into and exit out of the market.

91

31. ADVICE

Most investors will realise just how much analysis work and due diligence is necessary in order to stand a good chance of picking investment funds that are likely to outperform over the longer term and may therefore decide that they would prefer to seek some professional help and advice in the whole investment fund selection process and possibly in the ongoing management of portfolios thereafter as well.

How can investors find suitable investment specialists and what are the questions they should ask when they do?

First, when seeking investment advice from a financial adviser, you should ascertain the skills, experience and qualifications of the adviser.

Just as with say the legal profession, where the term solicitor will cover a wide range of varying skills and specialist knowledge, in areas ranging through litigation, family law, corporate finance, mergers and acquisitions, wills and probate, asylum, employment law and discrimination cases, the term financial adviser also covers a wide range of skills and specialist knowledge. From pension advice through to Inheritance Tax mitigation, divorce related work through to auto enrolment, cash-flow management through to family protection and life assurance ... and a variety of other specialist areas. As well as of course investment advice and investment portfolio management.

Just as some lawyers will try and offer a broad spread of services, so will the majority of financial advisers.

However I would suggest that in nearly all walks of professional life, a specialist is more likely to help lead you to a better outcome than a general practitioner.

Personally I wouldn't expect my GP to perform heart surgery on me. I would expect him/her to refer me to a specialist. A heart specialist or surgeon in this case. Equally I wouldn't go to a general practice, high street firm of solicitors, advertising conveyancing and/or wills and probate etc, to advise me on say a complex corporate merger or business acquisition. I would seek out a lawyer specialising in corporate finance.

.... and so it is with financial advice.

At an early stage in the in the engagement process, you should ask the adviser if they are an investment specialist or not. If the answer is yes then you may wish to ask a few questions to ascertain experience and qualifications.

Amongst the questions I would ask a potential investment adviser are:

Q. "How much client investment money do you currently have under management?"

(Generally speaking, I would suggest the higher the better, as successful advising in the field of investment and particularly in the subsequent portfolio management, tends to increase assets under management. The better the outcome achieved for you by an investment adviser, the more likely you are to recommend your friends and colleagues to that adviser. An adviser with a relatively small amount of clients' investments to manage might indicate a limited amount of experience or success, although it is fair to say there is no precise science around this).

Q. "How often are investments reviewed?"

(There should be a structure in place with investments being reviewed and discussed with you on a regular basis).

Q. "Do you have a bias towards passive investing or active management and why?"

(I would expect an investment specialist to be more involved in active management than passive investing, although any adviser should give consideration to both regimes).

Q. "Do you use a quantitative and/or qualitative analysis? If so, please explain them to me?"

(If they don't or can't explain this, I would suggest you find another adviser who is an investment specialist).

Q. "How do you measure alpha and beta?"

(If they don't or can't explain this, I would suggest you find another adviser who can demonstrate that they are an investment specialist).

Q. "What circumstances would trigger a sell recommendation?"

(There should be a clearly defined process laid down).

Q. *"Do you personally meet with the fund managers on a regular basis?"*

(Although not a fundamental requirement, analysis of a fund will often involve an understanding of facts which cannot clearly be ascertained from a fund's factsheet alone. Meeting a manager face to face, helps build intelligence on the fund which can be very useful, such as an understanding of the manager's particular style, for instance whether they adopt a macro, top down approach to stock selection, or whether they are very much stock pickers, utilising a bottom up approach allows. Their experience in the market and the length of time the fund's performance can be attributed to the individual manager).

Q. *"What qualifications of a specific investment nature do you hold?"*

(Although not exclusively, investment professionals are most likely to hold qualifications issued by one of a couple of organisations, including the Chartered Institute of Securities and Investments (CISI) where you will be looking for either MCSI (Member) or FCSI (fellow). The Investment Management Certificate (IMC) is the most widely recognised qualification of its kind in the UK, with over 15,000 investment professionals having successfully studied for the examination. Formerly issued by the Institute of Investment Management and Research, the awarding organisation of the IMC is now CFA UK).

You should also ask for a copy of the investment process they use. This should be clearly articulated and well documented. If it isn't, then to me that would be a **'red flag'**.

You need to find out whether or not they intend to manage the whole investment process themselves 'in-house' *(such a process would normally include the research of the whole market, the subsequent fund selection process, implementation of the investment purchases necessary to build a suitable portfolio and possibly some form of ongoing portfolio management thereafter).*

If not, are they intending to outsource to an investment specialist, such as a discretionary fund manager?. Or are they just going to place your investment in say a managed fund?. The latter might be fine for smaller investments, say up to £10,000. But for a portfolio of meaningful size, it is likely your interests will be better served by a portfolio of different investment funds, put together to meet your specific needs and objectives, risk profile and capacity for loss.

Having your financial adviser outsource to a specialist is perfectly acceptable, so long as you understand that there will be another tier of charges (*with both the financial adviser and the investment specialist each being paid for their respective work and services*). It is therefore important that you agree the specific work which is to be undertaken by each party in respect of the different charges they are making and you are absolutely clear as to 'who is doing what' for their money.

For instance, an adviser will probably need to undertake a comprehensive gathering of information exercise, relating to your specific circumstances, needs and objectives. This will usually also involve some form of assessment of your attitude to risk and your tolerance or capacity for loss.

Armed with all this information the non-investment specialist financial adviser can now undertake some form of due diligence, before deciding on which is the most suitable investment specialist or discretionary fund manager (DFM) to introduce you to, in order to meet your needs.

Since the Retail Distribution Review (RDR) became effective at the beginning of 2013, there has been a marked increase in the number of what might be referred to as generalist financial advisers, engaging with investment specialists to manage their clients' portfolios on their behalf, rather than advising directly on the monies themselves. Many such advisers have either recognised they don't have the necessary specialist skills and/or experience themselves to be able to select investment funds and construct portfolios successfully.

As I have said though, a concern is that such outsourcing by financial advisers is usually adding another tier of fees, so you must be sure you are **getting value for money** through such outsourcing. Arguably there can be merit in dealing with an adviser that has specialist investment skills in-house, as that will save additional fees which would otherwise be charged by DFMs and the like.

An investment specialist will have a repeatable and sustainable investment process and this should be articulated and documented for you, so that you are able to discuss and assess the extent of their processes.

KEY SUMMARY POINT

On balance, a good adviser or investment specialist 'should pay their way', with fees being more than offset by any tax savings they can introduce through good product recommendation and/or excess performance over an agreed benchmark.

WHAT ARE 5 THINGS YOU SHOULD PROBABLY AVOID WHEN PICKING INVESTMENT FUNDS?

1. MAKING NARROW BASED INVESTMENT DECISIONS

One of the things that have held me in good stead over the years, both personally and professionally, has been not to take things at face value. In my business life I believe it is vital to weigh up all the facts before making a judgement. Carry out comprehensive due diligence, ignore the 'noise' of the market, be aware of and pay attention to sentiment but act on fundamentals.

How many people can you think of, have jumped to the wrong conclusion over something, acted on a tiny piece of evidence or even just 'village gossip' and made 2+2 add up to 57, then have done something they've regretted?. I know I can say I know a few!!

Experience of life has taught me to listen well to my instincts but act on evidence.

When I was going through my pilot training many, many years ago, there were two things I was taught by my instructor in particular which have stuck with me ever since.

The first is that you should always rely on your instruments and the factual data they provide, over any gut feeling. This was mainly so that if you found yourself in what might be referred to as a 'weather predicament', to such an extent that you no longer had visual contact with the ground, then you <u>must</u> accept the data your instruments were giving you, regarding vital aspects such as the attitude of the plane (*i.e. are the wings level?*). Rather than attempting to fly the plane to the attitude that you <u>think</u> it is in ... such as straight and level flight, you must fly exactly in accordance with what the actual data is telling you.

My instructor would prove time and time again how instincts could let pilots down. He did this by taking control of the aircraft whilst we were in flight and asking me to place a special mask over my eyes which limited my vision to the instrument panel only with no external visual references to be seen at all.

Then I was asked to close my eyes and he would put the aircraft into a particular attitude (*e.g. climbing to the left or maybe descending to the right*). He would ask me to interpret the attitude of the plane from my 'feelings' alone (*with no visual sense input at all now*). The answer was usually and most surprisingly, wrong, because of course the body is accustomed to the primary sense of sight to determine something like this. When that sense is taken away, then believe it or not, the resulting human instinct can play tricks on you.

One could safely assume a partially sighted or blind person would probably do much better in such a situation (*as their body would have become accustomed to using other senses to determine something like attitude*). But then it's fair to say that there are probably not many partially sighted pilots!

The second point, particularly applicable in say visual navigation, was that wherever possible you should always take at least **two** and preferably three reference points before making a decision. The second and possibly third reference points reinforce the first of course. By only taking one, say a particular road or railway line or a small village etc, then there is a good chance that you could actually have made a mistake and in fact it wasn't the road or railway line position you thought it was!. By cross referencing to a second and sometimes even a third reference point, you would either confirm or dismiss your judgement which was based on the first alone.

Well I believe these two principles (*act on facts and preferably cross reference those facts*) carry across very well into investment decisions and due diligence as well. Whilst accepting that gut instinct is often based on experience and that experience is a hugely beneficial asset, you should cross reference that with at least a couple of specific pieces of fundamental data. Check and then check again.

For instance, one of the biggest mistakes amateur investors make, is to base their buying decisions purely on past investment performance.

By its very nature, investment performance is 'rear facing'. It tells us where we've been, not where we're going. For sure it can give you an insight into one important facet of an investment fund.

But as I talked about earlier, in any event in many ways it is HOW that performance has been delivered, which is as important as the finite figure itself. In the past investment companies were prone to promote funds by advertising in the press etc, after the market, the particular sector the fund operated in, or the fund itself, had delivered a period of excellent growth. Invariably funds were seen to launch at or near to the top of a particular market. With the benefit of hindsight, in the case of many fund launches the best of the growth in that sector was already behind it.

Investors bought in at the top and then of course became somewhat disillusioned with the subsequent results.

An excellent example of how investment groups attracted large sums of money from investors at the wrong time, was in the period leading up to the dot.com bubble in the late 1990s and very early 2000s. Valuations of 'tech' stocks at that time were at best, stretched and at worst, massively over-priced and yet investment groups continued to market their technology funds right up until the time the bubble burst in the spring of 2000, unfortunately leaving investors nursing heavy losses in the aftermath.

The benefit of hindsight is of course a wonderful thing but had some basic valuation criteria been applied to these stocks and the head had ruled investment decisions, rather than the heart, then much of the fall-out might have been averted.

KEY SUMMARY POINT

It's always beneficial to use some due diligence in the fund selection process, other than just past performance data.

2. BIASED INFORMATION

- ARE YOU BEING 'SOLD TO' BY A BUSINESS WHICH CAN ONLY MARKET ITS OWN FUNDS? ...

- OR ARE YOU BEING 'ADVISED WITH TOTAL IMPARTIALITY'?

It is fair to say that independent and impartially sourced analytical material relating to investments, will nearly always be more reliable than the marketing material offered by an organisation promoting a particular investment product or investment fund. The 'promoter' is far more likely to put a 'gloss' or 'positive spin' on some of the attributes of an investment and naturally, may not be that forthcoming about any negatives!.

If you are 'buying' an investment product rather than making your own decision to invest, then ascertain whether or not the person or company you are buying the investment product from, actually works for or is associated with the organisation itself *(and can therefore only promote products from that company)*, OR, has access to the whole market place.

A question you should ask yourself if dealing with a company that promotes its own products is, how likely are they going to be to recommend that you sell when things go wrong? *(such as a fund consistently underperforming its peer group)*. Realistically, the answer is 'highly unlikely'.

If for instance the organisation you have bought the investment from, put you into a fund which let's say specialised in investing in UK small companies … and after a reasonable period of time, say two to three years, whilst UK small companies generally might be performing very well, the fund you have been persuaded to invest in is regularly appearing at the bottom of the league table of all UK smaller company funds, be realistic and ask yourself the question *"How likely am I to be told to sell and take my investment elsewhere?"*.

Indeed some would suggest that the vested interests which populate financial services have been one of the primary causes of the various mis-selling scandals over the years. Take away vested interests and you are much more likely to get a better outcome. The removal of remuneration by way of commission, as part of the introduction of the RDR in January 2013, was a huge step forward in bringing about professionalism and also attempted to clarify the status of those providing advice, be it independent or restricted.

KEY SUMMARY POINT

Take time to understand whether your source of information or advice is truly impartial and independent, or from the very company or associate of the company promoting the investment.

3. NEGATIVE ALPHA

As we referred to at point **19**, page 67, earlier in this guide, alpha is an important technical ratio which enables us to ascertain how much value a fund manager is adding, over and above a suitable market index or benchmark return. As such it is a very useful indicator to both the investor and a professional investment specialist alike.

Conversely therefore, a fund with negative alpha characteristics will suggest that the fund has actually underperformed and will have taken away some or all of the market return. It might therefore be best avoided, particularly if there is evidence that this has happened on a regular basis.

Arguably a monkey throwing darts at the dartboard might have done better!

Bear in mind though that a perfectly good fund can slip into negative alpha territory on a temporary basis, if certain market conditions go against it. This is one of the reasons that one's timeframe for analysis shouldn't be too short term otherwise you can end up chipping and chopping holdings, incurring costs in the process, when a longer term strategy would have been the preferred option.

4. UNREGULATED FUNDS

This is a huge generalisation but I would certainly advocate **buyer beware** in the area of unregulated collective investment schemes (*hereinafter referred to as UCIS*) and near substitutes, collectively known as non-mainstream pooled investments (*hereinafter referred to as NMPIs*). A NMPI may include a Qualified Investors Scheme (*hereinafter referred to as QIS*) or a Special Purpose Vehicle (*hereinafter referred to as SPV*).

The types of fund which can constitute a UCIS are wide. A UCIS will lack regulatory control as to the type of assets the fund can invest in. There would be no rules for instance on diversification (*meaning a fund could have just a single asset held in it, which is in itself an additional risk*). Rules are in place with regulated collective investment schemes to do with diversification, to ensure a prudent spread of risk.

Furthermore UCIS are not subject to rules or constraints on the fund's ability to borrow, resulting in some of them being **highly geared** (*i.e. there could be high levels of borrowing within the structure of the scheme*).

Typical of UCIS are funds investing in land banks, overseas property developments, or non-traditional areas such as carbon credits.

They may be established, operated by and/or managed in the UK or in any jurisdiction outside of the UK.

UCIS can be complex and opaque, with various corporate structures and parties involved in the management and promotion of such schemes. The legal complexities are often difficult to navigate through and you can therefore struggle to identify the true legal structure of the schemes, as well as the investment strategy and risks to investors.

The most **significant drawback** of investing in **such a scheme is that you are likely to have little or no protection if things go wrong.** The compensation arrangements in place in the UK simply do <u>not</u> cover unregulated schemes (*unless you have been advised to invest in such a scheme, or induced to engage in investment activity, by a regulated adviser, who will then be responsible for ensuring things such as suitability*).

Likewise you will not be able to engage the services of the **Financial Ombudsman** either (*again unless you have been advised to invest in such a scheme, or induced to engage in investment activity, by a regulated adviser*).

Additional significant disadvantages of investing in a UCIS can include much **higher risks** in the vast majority of cases, probably **liquidity constraints** (*i.e., you may not be able to get your money out when you want to*), **high costs** and possibly **tax implications** too.

Whilst it is fair to say that some unregulated investments carry less risk than others, in general terms, one should generally be particularly wary of unregulated investment funds and I would even go so far as to say, be somewhat wary of <u>some</u> of the firms that promote them, given the potential dangers to investors.

Extreme care needs to be taken when investing into a UCIS or near substitute via a regulated product, such as a SIPP. Some confusion has arisen in the past with investors believing that the underlying investments in the SIPP (*including any UCIS therefore*) were covered by regulation and therefore enjoyed a degree of potential regulatory protection, because the SIPP itself was regulated.

This situation is unfortunately **not** the case. Just because the SIPP provider is regulated does **not** automatically mean that the underlying UCIS will be. As such the aforementioned **lack of investor protection** or right to compensation will still be evident regarding the underlying UCIS itself.

Likewise extreme care needs to be taken if any 'adviser' or 'promoter' of the UCIS suggests that you invest into it by way of signing an **'execution only'** statement.

This means you would be asked to sign something stipulating that the investment wasn't actually recommended or promoted to you at all (!), but that **you made the sole decision to invest, without receiving any advice at any stage.** Being asked to sign an Execution Only statement in conjunction with a UCIS or near substitute should, in itself, be a **'red flag'**.

110

The **Financial Conduct Authority** (*hereinafter referred to as FCA*) regards UCIS as niche products and almost certainly, (*they specifically state*) **inappropriate for 'ordinary retail investors'.** As such they cannot be promoted to the general public in the UK but can be to certain categories of investor, mostly based around being sophisticated investors or those who are deemed to be of high net worth (*hereinafter referred to as HNW*). The regulators will have clear definitions as to what constitutes either a sophisticated investor or is deemed to be of HNW.

If you are not sure as to whether or not a particular fund is regulated, you can check the regulators' websites. Established on 1ˢᵗ April 2013, the FCA (*www.the-fca.org.co.uk*) is the conduct regulator for some 56,000 financial services firms and the financial markets in the UK, as well being the prudential regulator for some 24,000 of those firms.

The Prudential Regulation Authority (*hereinafter referred to as PRA*) (*www.bankofengland.co.uk/pra*) is the prudential regulator of some 1,700 banks, building societies, credit unions, insurers and designated major investment firms.

KEY SUMMARY POINT

Investing in a UCIS or near substitute, greatly increases your chance of losing money. It is a case of buyer definitely be beware.

5. CLOSET INDEX TRACKERS

This is a colloquial term used to describe a fund which is ostensibly an actively managed fund (*with the higher management fees associated with active management*) but where the fund manager is in fact taking very few 'bets' away from the stocks that are included in a particular index associated with the fund. So one ends up with a fund that looks very much like an index tracker, performs and behaves like an index tracker, but which carries the higher charges associated with active fund management. Arguably you would get better value by investing in an index tracker than such a fund.

Luckily there are techniques which can be employed to spot closet index trackers and thus avoid paying higher charges unnecessarily. One such technique for instance would be to look for a fund with a very high R-squared value (*see 23. **R-Squared**).

KEY SUMMARY POINT

There are I believe, many closet trackers out there, effectively replicating a relevant index and yet charging investors fees at a level for active management. You need to be able to utilise appropriate technical indicators to recognise these funds and thereby potentially save yourself unnecessary fees.

INDEX

ABOUT THE AUTHOR

Richard Jennings is the senior portfolio manager with JNJ Financial Management, (*www.jnjfinancial.co.uk*) has **over 30 years' experience** in analysing collective investment funds on behalf of clients and a very successful track record in constructing and managing investment portfolios.

Generally recognised as an **investment specialist** and highly regarded by his peer group, he counts several ex or retired investment professionals and stockbrokers amongst his own personal client bank.

Frequently asked for his opinion on investment matters by national newspapers, he was one of only a handful of investment specialists in the U.K. to sit on the former BBC TV Ceefax Unit Trust Panel.

Richard is also the author of *'Inheritance Tax – A Definitive Guide'*.

Lightning Source UK Ltd.
Milton Keynes UK
UKOW07f1718041116

286789UK00012B/1/P

9 780995 634800